MARVELOUS MAZES

MARVELOUS MAZES

Juliet & Charles Snape

Harry N. Abrams, Inc. • Publishers

ISBN 0-8109-2576-1

Copyright © 1994 Juliet & Charles Snape

First published in Great Britain in 1994 by Julia MacRae Books,
an imprint of Random House UK Limited, under the title *The Fantastic Maze Book*

Published in 1994 by Harry N. Abrams, Incorporated, New York

Printed in Hong Kong

Introduction

A maze is a deliberately confusing series of paths or passages leading to a specific point and designed to make life difficult, with lots of false turns, dead ends, and traps. Mazes are very ancient — in Greek mythology the Minotaur was imprisoned in a maze — and they can still sometimes be found in the gardens of great houses and estates. Mazes are fun, but they can be tricky.

The mazes in this book have been specially created to stretch your imagination and test your skill. They are not marked with *Starts* and *Finishes*, and they do not always begin on the left and end on the right. Each maze has a different setting, and finding where to begin can be part of the challenge. Be prepared to go right inside the pictures: into rooms, behind pillars, through doors, up ropes, down steps, and even into a boat. . . .

There are solutions at the back of the book, but don't look at them unless you are truly lost. It is much more exciting to find the way for yourself!

Juliet & Charles

Journey through the Hills

Travel through the dangerous hills to reach
the cottage.

Stranger in the City

The guide book tells you to visit the palace with the four towers. From the city gates, can you find the way through the old town to the palace?

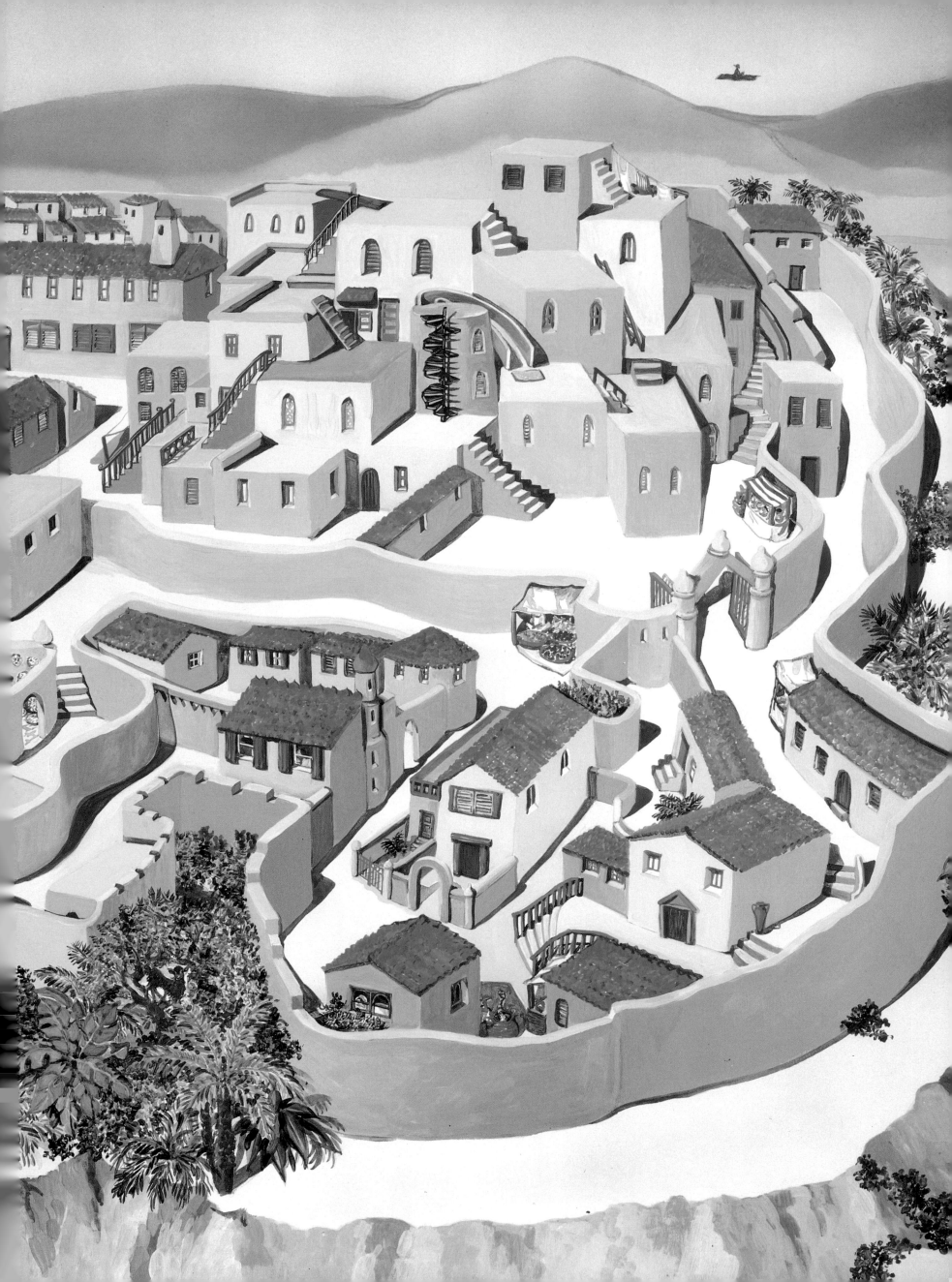

Canoe Trip

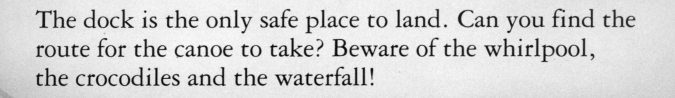

The dock is the only safe place to land. Can you find the route for the canoe to take? Beware of the whirlpool, the crocodiles and the waterfall!

Tree Houses

The green pixie has been invited to tea by the tree fairy. Can you help him find the way to her through the tree houses?

Escape from the Castle

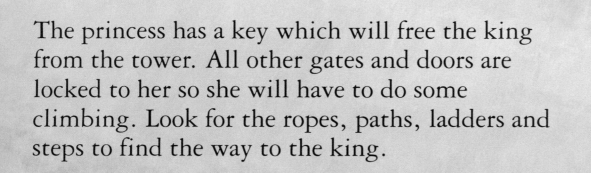

The princess has a key which will free the king
from the tower. All other gates and doors are
locked to her so she will have to do some
climbing. Look for the ropes, paths, ladders and
steps to find the way to the king.

Ghost Hunting

Creep in at the side door and find your way to
the ghost's hiding place.

Troll World

Tolly Troll gets out of bed. How does she sneak outside to play in the snow before school starts?

Treasure Hunt

The pirate wants to find a way across the bridges to the treasure on top of Blue Mountain. How does he do it?

The Enchanted Forest

The route through the enchanted forest is full of dangers,
but there are bats to warn you along the way,
and at the end a boat to carry you to safety.

Tracks and Trains

The blue train has to go to the downtown station and
the red train has to go to the seashore station.
Which tracks should they follow?

Crazy Paving

Go down the steps on the left and, stepping only on the paving stones, find a path to the fountain, then cross the square to the steps on the other side. You must keep to the same pattern of a circle followed by a square.

Pirate Ship

It is time for the cabin boy to climb the middle mast to the lookout platform. Can you find where he is sleeping on the floor, and the route he must take?

Possible Solutions

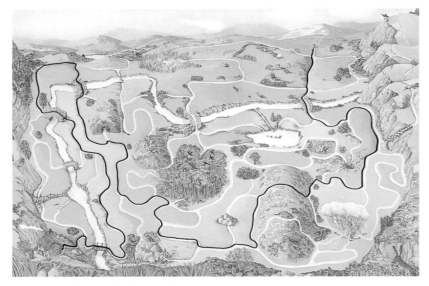

Journey through the Hills

Stranger in the City

Canoe Trip

Tree Houses

Escape from the Castle

Ghost Hunting